The Good, the Bad, the Mother-in-Law

Stories of Good and (Alarmingly) Bad Relationships

Kenis Dunne

The Good, the Bad, the Mother-in-Law
By Kenis Dunne

Copyright 2020 by Kenis Dunne
Cover Copyright 2020 by Dunnes Publishing
Bunny Ears Illustration by KC Palma
Cover Design by Ginny Glass, Untreed Reads

ISBN-978-0-578-73982-3

Also available in ebook format.

Printed in the United States of America.

www.kenisdunne.com

Thank you to all my friends, family and co-workers who trusted me with their mother-in-law experiences and anecdotes. Some of your stories are offered here verbatim (yes, as promised, I changed the names to protect your familial relationships). Others are paraphrased synopses and mash-ups of countless conversations on the subject of mothers-in-law, good and not-so-good.

Thank you also to the savvy daughters-in-law who offered commentary in the form of life lessons: Karolyn Baker, Megan Langenhuysen, KC Palma, Katie O'Malley and Shannon Rush-Call. With a particular shout out to my mentor-in-chief, K.D. Sullivan of Untreed Reads.

And, one last thank you to Pat Christie, who gave me hours of storytelling time in a Los Gatos coffee shop at the very start.

Contents

Every Book Needs a Cheat Sheet, Right?

This book is a collection of stories about mothers-in-law as told by daughters-in-law with a few sons-in-law mixed in. Because so many of the stories begged a lesson to be learned (morals to the stories), I enlisted the help of several savvy daughters-in-law to add commentaries.

Meet the Cadre of Savvy Daughters-in-Law

Thank you to the fun and sassy daughters-in-law who set the records straight and offered their own words of wisdom.

Karolyn Baker – Mother of 3. A daughter-in-law since 2012.

Megan Langenhuysen – Mother of 1. A daughter-in-law since 2015.

Katie O'Malley – Mother of 3. A daughter-in-law since 2010.

KC Palma – Mother of 2. A daughter-in-law since 2016.

Shannon Rush-Call – Mother of 3. Our book's veteran daughter-in-law, with 22 years of experience.

Book Speak: MIL? DIL? SIL?

Throughout the book you will see references to MIL for mother-in-law and DIL for daughter-in-law. I've also tossed in an occasional SIL for son-in-law. Apologies to the punctuation purists for using MILs when referring to multiple mothers-in-law.

I also added my own observations to introduce each story. And make sure to look for tips from pro mothers-in-law — offering extra help and humor along the way. Here's a sampling:

Your history is not her future

I'm no doctor, but I'm confident we have no business drawing conclusions about someone else's pregnancy.

As she told it, my mother-in-law had been depressed during each of her four pregnancies and in the four or five months following each birth. Given she had four children in five years, I calculate that she was pretty much depressed for five years straight. So when I was pregnant with our first baby, she predicted that I would be a mess during the pregnancy, which I wasn't. Then when she came to stay with us after the baby was born, she constantly recalled her own post-delivery woes. If I was testy or even sighed out loud, she was almost happy – "See, you have the depression, too." Truthfully, she could have *made* me depressed. *–Lindsay, "I'm Good" DIL*

> My introductory thoughts!

> Moments in time, as told to me

Life Lesson from a Savvy DIL

First, what were you thinking letting your mother-in-law stay with you after the baby was born? There's a rule about messing with a postpartum mom. Unsolicited input — especially negative — on pregnancy or mental/emotional state is never welcome. *–KC*

> Advice and commentary from daughters-in-law who've been there

01

The Thing About MILs and DILs

There is nothing quite like the relationship between a mother-in-law and her daughter-in-law. And vice versa. The stories in this book run the gamut — from cautionary tales to wonderfully memorable.

This all began 34 years ago

I was a young fiancée, then a bride, like nearly all of my friends before me. We talked a lot about adjusting to our new lives — at first as wives, and later as mothers. A common topic — especially when combined with a glass or two of wine — was our mothers-in-law. We bolstered each other over unjust criticisms and I said/she said skirmishes. No matter how minor or egregious the story, we promised each other that we would always remember how these interactions felt and *never* do the same when we became mothers-in-law.

Then, somehow, we fast-forwarded through 34 years of life. As our children began to pair up and move into their own marriages and partnerships, we actually couldn't remember specifically what was so terrible about our mothers-in-law, or why their behavior had mattered so much. I had this nagging suspicion that such thinking was exactly what got our own mothers-in-law into trouble with us back in the day.

I decided to do a refresher course on the topic of MILs with the ready population of young women (and men) I worked with. I asked them about their mothers-in-law, looking for stories that would inspire, as well as serve as cautionary tales of behavior to avoid. To be honest, sometimes their stories of micro-inequities sounded to me like whining. (I had to forcibly stop myself one time from interjecting with, "And how much exactly are you paying your mother-in-law to watch your kids every Tuesday?" I knew the answer was zero.)

I started observing how my peers navigated their roles as mothers-in-law and grandmothers. I began to see both sides of the stories, something I had never thought to do with my own mother-in-law.

I hope you enjoy the stories as much as I enjoyed collecting them.

02

Those Were the (Early) Days, My Friend

Oh, those early days of a relationship. As the song goes, they only have eyes for each other. And not for you, the potential mother-in-law. Whenever and however you are brought into their circle, be thoughtful in your approach. Just as you are forming your own first impressions of this new special someone, they are doing the very same concerning you. Be welcoming and accepting from the very start.

Assume positive intent

I can't imagine that momma thought this one through.

We arrived for the holidays with our new puppy in hand. We were staying for a long weekend, and had verified that it was OK to bring the puppy, who was house-trained and generally well-behaved. Instead of being concerned about the dog's behavior, you know what his mother wanted her son to know? That if we were to break up, since he had paid for the adoption costs, that he should have a written agreement so he could keep the dog. Merry damn Christmas to you too. –Lexi, Offended DIL

 Life Lesson from a Savvy DIL

Ouch! If you two were married, that's a pretty huge undercut to the relationship, but if you're dating, I'd give her the benefit of the doubt that she is "just" looking out for her son and his feelings. Rude as the comment was—act mature and respectful and show her you're here to stay! –Karolyn

Comparisons only work when favorable

You had me at "hippie photographer."

The second time I had dinner at my husband's home, Jon's mom brought up his ex-girlfriend. This was an ex he had dated when he was something like 19 years old (he was 32 at the time of this dinner). She asked Jon about how the ex was doing, and whether or not she was still doing photography, and said "I really liked Chelsea. When are we going to get to see her again?" Big surprise, that was just the start of her insensitivity.

My future father-in-law, thankfully, came to the rescue by defending me, pointing out I was a successful attorney and that he was incredibly happy to have me there instead of the "hippie photographer." –Leslie, *Incomparable DIL*

Life Lesson from a Savvy DIL

Your father-in-law is where it's at. Thank him, hug him, bond with him. Ignore your MIL. I'd also enlist your husband in managing his mother. Her behavior, in this situation, was callous. The more he can be clear with her how he expects you to be treated as a part of the family, the better. Let the two men manage her insensitivity while you stay in the background. –Shannon

Tip from a Pro MIL

Where to stay?

If your kids aren't local, when you first travel to stay with the new couple, figure out a protocol before that first visit. Do they want you to stay at their house? Is there room for you comfortably? Would a motel close by be better for all? If finances allow, offer to stay at a local hotel.

Be mindful...this could be "the one"

As I heard this story, I wondered what the true back story might be. Good intentions poorly executed? Exuberance gone bad?

James and I were "a thing." We spent most of our off-work time together. We had not introduced each other to our parents, however. My story is about how I met my future mother-in-law. Apparently, she was annoyed that she hadn't met her son's new girlfriend. One Saturday morning, she arrived at his doorstep, ostensibly to see if he wanted to go get coffee. She immediately spied my laptop and purse on the coffee table, and strongly "suggested" that he bring me out to meet her. And off he went to do so. I was sound asleep. I was a bit hungover. No makeup. No clothing for that matter. But I did the best I could with my hair and threw on a sweatshirt and leggings. She was fairly pleasant, we chatted amicably, and she went on her way. I assumed all had gone well. Later, she told James she was quite offended that I didn't take the time to dress for the day and meet her properly. Knowing that she has that side of her, I've definitely kept her at a distance. That's not my nature, but I don't trust her. *–Maya, Fooled Me Once DIL*

 **Life Lesson from a Savvy DIL**

Don't overthink it so soon. I fully agree she forced this intro at an inappropriate time, and if she had high expectations of what it would be like to meet you, she should have provided more runway for you to prepare. However, give it time to get to know her. Some of these trivial things she values (like having lipstick on) could be generational and won't impact the broader relationship you could potentially build. Don't write her off yet, especially if this is your children's future babysitter...errrr...I mean, grandmother! *–Katie*

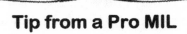

Tip from a Pro MIL

Plan early for holiday protocols

Don't procrastinate on how you will handle the holidays.
Think it through and relay your preferences. Don't wait to
just let the events or milestones unfold because that's when
feelings get hurt. You're not going to get it all your way —
usually there are two extended families (at least) involved.
Know what's all-important, and be willing to compromise.

Fit pitching, not a solid strategy

You know those times when you simply cannot help but chime in? I'm betting this was one of those. At least Faz stepped in immediately.

We were planning to live together, part of our grand plan to eventually marry, but realized we were too young. Also, who knows, right? Maybe the reality of living with only each other, as compared to our many roommates, would cause us to change our minds about committing to a lifetime together. When Faz announced the part about us living together, his mother pitched a fit. She immediately asked if I would be carrying my own weight in paying for rent and expenses. I'm not really sure that's any of her business. To his credit, Faz talked to her privately and got a reluctant agreement that she would not comment about this anymore. But it's definitely cast a taint on my relationship with her. *—Stacy, Weight-Bearing DIL*

Life Lesson from a Savvy DIL

Stacy, your MIL is someone with whom you will have a lifelong relationship. It's totally possible her concern about equal financial contribution is coming from a previous relationship that her son had where money was an issue. Or maybe a challenge she was forced to navigate herself. Her concern might actually have nothing to do with you, per se. I'd suggest you let this one go, and get to work building a relationship with your MIL for the long-term. (And also thank Faz for stepping in on your behalf.) *—Shannon*

Jump on in, the family's fine

There are a couple of stories like this one. My take-away? We mothers-in-law sometimes just can't win. Don't overstep, don't underperform.

In most ways, I quite like my mother-in-law. What I do not appreciate is that from the very start, when she visits, she can't see when I need help. I work full-time, so I'm frazzled much of the time. What I want to say to her is this: "Help me out please. See a pile of laundry? By all means, fold. Dirty dishes? By all means, wash them. It's OK to focus at the surface level. I'm not expecting you to pull the trash cans out. But don't stand mute in the kitchen, waiting to ask me where the spoons are. It's fine to open a drawer to check. You are FAMILY, not a special guest." *–Tammy, Frazzled DIL*

 Life Lesson from a Savvy DIL

Amen! I hear you, but keep in mind she may "think" she's respecting your boundaries by not helping herself in your home. This could be generational, or simply her style, so I'd suggest breaking the ice on this topic. Next time she's over, show your vulnerable, frazzled self and say, "Sorry, life is nuts in this house. Honestly, if you're up for it, I'd love some help. There are no boundaries here; you're family! Would you mind helping me with the dishes? It would mean so much to me." See how she responds; she simply may have needed your approval to jump in. If this offends her, then she can go find her own damn spoon. *–Katie*

"Take your cue from whoever is in charge of the household routines. If the house is pin-neat, probably a good idea to make your bed in the mornings. Rinse your coffee mug and put it in the dishwasher. It's not a Bed & Breakfast, it's your child's home."

–Unknown

New holiday traditions? Wait...what?!

Darby's story could have been worse. At least neither family was abandoned entirely in that exciting first holiday gathering. I'm five years in, and my daughter and husband still fly in for Christmas Eve, then take the first morning flight back to Portland. I now realize how lucky I am.

My husband's parents have a big house with a gigantic dining room table, which is where, for as many years as they have had children, they host Christmas Eve dinner, game night and gift exchange. The problem is that my parents have a similar, albeit less lavish, Christmas Eve tradition. Around about Thanksgiving of our first holiday as a married couple, we had one of those "Wait...what?" conversations where each of us assumed we would be continuing with our own family's Christmas Eve celebrations. I'd like to say it worked out fine in the end, but it did not. The situation was made all the more exasperating because both sets
of parents refused to even consider letting go of their long-standing traditions. In the end, we each spent our first Christmas Eve with our own families, but without each other. *–Darby, Holiday-Weary DIL*

Life Lesson from a Savvy DIL

This is ultimately the choice of the DIL and SIL. I may be the stubborn one, but there doesn't actually need to be a compromise; choose the one you want to go to. Don't ever expect people to change their traditions to fit your plans. When this came up for us, we just decided to make our own tradition. Now we try to spend every Thanksgiving in a tropical location, alone. Neither family is upset! (Or they both are, equally.) *–Megan*

03

It's Official — They're Engaged!

Now you have an official role: mother of the bride or groom. Do your best to watch from the sidelines. Offer to help, rather than jump into their planning process. It's your time to shine with love, support and an ever-positive vibe.

Social graces are not defined by your generation

While I question her delivery, I tend to agree with Vickie on this one. Just saying.

Vickie, my mother-in-law, got married before Amazon and online gift registries. So, in "her day," everyone brought wrapped presents to the bridal and baby showers. Ahead of my second bridal shower, because she had seen a "profound lack of social grace" at my first shower when guests arrived empty-handed, she went ahead and sent a separate "helpful" email to my guests, suggesting that they bring their gifts so I had something to open at the party. I found out what she had done when my maid of honor clued me in. The damage was done, so I didn't address it, but I'm still annoyed. –*Cory, Annoyed DIL*

 Life Lesson from a Savvy DIL

This sounds like an honest misunderstanding! She may not have handled it in the best way, but she wanted you to have a great party and experience the joy and excitement of opening those gifts. She wanted your day to be special! Let this one go. –*Karolyn*

With this ring, my mom and I thee wed

I'm nearly certain this story is about good intentions gone awry.

My now husband and I went together to look at rings. I fell in love with two (one-of-a-kind) antique rings. One being slightly more expensive. The antique dealer's website had links for both rings, so for weeks (probably months) I was checking to see if the rings were still available. One day, the less-expensive (though still gorgeous) ring was gone. I was *praying* he had purchased it. But months went on, and no proposal. Finally, he did propose on a cliff above the ocean, with that beautiful one-of-a-kind ring.

Years later, he told me his mom went and bought the ring behind his back. She claimed she used the money she was going to give us for our wedding. I know many will say this was a kind gesture, but it has always left me slightly unsettled. Partially because *he* didn't get to pick which one to buy, and a bigger part because he may not have been ready to buy a ring at all!

Side note: Sometimes when friends get extravagant rings, my husband jokingly tells me, "Sorry my mom couldn't afford that ring for you." *–Christine, Unsettled DIL*

Life Lesson from a Savvy DIL

I agree that's an odd, fairly invasive approach. Especially that she didn't first confer with her son. Perhaps her logic was to take the ring off the market? At least you got the right ring AND a husband with a sense of humor. *–KC*

I see the real you

I'd like to fact-check the "wonderful partner" part. If he loves her, why share his mother's feelings about her?

I'm pretty awesome. I know that sounds arrogant, and I don't mean it to, but it is true. I'm a happy, healthy, nice-looking woman who has friends and family who love me. And now a wonderful partner who loves me just as I am. Imagine my surprise to learn from him that his mother *doesn't* like me...at all. I don't know why, and truthfully, does it matter? At this point, I'm not going to be changing up what has worked pretty darn well so far. But one day I may just tell her, "You're a wolf in sheep's clothing, and I see the real you." – *Jenelle, Royally Pissed Off DIL*

 Life Lesson from a Savvy DIL

Mmm, this is tough. It sounds like you have a strong sense of self-worth, not just because other people like you, but you like who you are in the world. Stay centered on that — continue being your awesome self, including in how you interact with your MIL. Then, someday, maybe she'll change her opinion about you. And, if she doesn't, you can decide if letting her know "she's a wolf in sheep's clothing" is truly aligned with the awesome person you say you are. –*Shannon*

"The first rule of a happy in-law
relationship is to diminish the
opportunities for discord."
–Ask Amy advice column

You Say, She Says. Who's Right?

~~~~~~

Engagement Ring Re-Gifting

Daughter-in-Law: My mother-in-law's original engagement ring was very modest but beautiful. It had a fairly large opal surrounded by teensy tiny diamond chips on a gold band. I loved that she gave it to her only son to give to me, since we were young and dirt-poor when we got married. I wore it for a few years, and then when our finances allowed, my husband bought me a new diamond engagement ring. I love the original one, too, for sentimental reasons, so I had the opal removed and made into a necklace. My mother-in-law was "offended to her very core." Her words. She asked for all the "parts" back (impossible given I had tossed the diamond chips.) She hurt my feelings and clearly, I hurt hers.

Mother-in-Law: For their engagement, I gifted my opal engagement ring to my son so he could give it to his girlfriend when they got engaged. I expected that she would be appreciative of the gesture and wear it for years. Instead, not even five years later, my son bought her a new ring. Rather than offering to return my ring — which had immense sentimental value to me — my daughter-in-law took it apart and made a necklace with the opal. She threw the band and diamonds away. I cannot get over this selfish and thoughtless act.

~~~~~~

04

Bells Will Be Ringing

Congratulations! You are about to graduate to the main stage: mother-in-law. As the wedding plans unfold, there are any number of opportunities for you to contribute to the celebration. And it's not just about the big day itself, but the myriad details and milestones that lead up to the wedding day. Planning for a wedding can be stressful for all involved – in particular, the bride and groom. Do all you can to bring your positive, nonjudgmental self to the process.

No, your poodle is not part of the plan

You have to admit, the wedding photos would have been fabulous.

I didn't want children at the wedding. There were no young kids in our family yet, so that meant no flower girls. My MIL thought the lack of "little voices" was a "damn shame." She offered to put a wreath on the family poodle, and they would walk her down the aisle. I thought her suggestion was not all that funny — a little joke gone wrong in my view. Turns out, she was serious and had ordered a dog collar wedding wreath. P.S.: The dog stayed home.
—Ashleigh, Poodle-less DIL

 Life Lesson from a Savvy DIL

Note to the MIL: No one loves your dog more than you. But a dog is not a replacement for a flower girl. This is the bride and groom's call, just as all of the wedding features. They might choose to walk down the aisle to heavy metal, and it isn't really anyone's business. Brides (and grooms) create the ceremony they want, so just nod and smile. —Megan

Smile sweetly; lie if you must

What a very lucky mother-in-law — that Miranda didn't hear about this on her big day.

All our friends were going to a pre-ceremony brunch, hosted the morning of our wedding by my soon-to-be mother-in-law at her house. I was off with my mom getting my hair and makeup done. When I arrived, the brunch was in full swing in the backyard, with my mother-in-law holding court in the kitchen with those "kids" she had known from the neighborhood. When I walked into the kitchen, I was greeted with a stunning silence — like I had just interrupted a private conversation that I wasn't to be privy to. Which is exactly what had happened. Fortunately, I didn't learn until months later that my mother-in-law was predicting a quick failure of our marriage, including specifics of why she felt I wasn't a good choice. Our friends told me that I hadn't interrupted anything, because they were all sitting in awkward disbelief
at the nature of the conversation when I waltzed in that morning.
—Miranda, Blissfully Ignorant DIL

Life Lesson from a Savvy DIL

MIL, chill out. You hate her? You think he's making a mistake? It is *his* mistake not yours. AND chances are, it isn't a mistake. You raised him, you were an example of a wife and mother to him, so trust yourself — and him. He probably chose someone more like you than you realize. Often, we are most resistant to people who are actually similar to us. If you want a lasting relationship with your DIL, your grandkids, and potentially your son, bottle that hatred right up. Fake it till you make it. *—Megan*

Beware the daughter-in-law scorned

There's really no easy way to spin this story. Chalk it up as yet another cautionary tale?

We were so very young when we got married. As in just out of high school. Back then, it didn't occur to me to stand up for myself (or my marriage) when it came to my mother-in-law. She was all over our marriage from the get-go — intervening and pronouncing what was best for her son. I didn't know it then, but that would be the pattern of our relationship. She was right, I was wrong. Her son (her favorite) was the only thing that mattered, followed next by her grandchildren. That was the pattern until the day I walked out on her favored son, and took those favored grandchildren to build a happier life together. I wasn't 18 years old anymore. Do I hate her? Yes, I do. But do I punish her for how she treated me? Yes, I do. — *Alma, Long Memory DIL*

 Life Lesson from a Savvy DIL

Ah, the classic bad mother-in-law. Too bad she then got to think she was right about the marriage, huh? Seriously, though, MILs: No daughter-in-law in the history of daughters-in-law wants your unsolicited input on her marriage. If you ask your son to choose which of you is right, and your son takes your side over your daughter-in-law, you've just chipped away at the trust and strength of that marriage and guaranteed a tough or impossible road to a good relationship with your daughter-in-law. Stay out of their marriage. –KC

Wedding attire is off-limits

I'd say pick your battles, momma. And dress color really shouldn't be on the list.

My mother-in-law and I had a fairly big disagreement over the color of the bridesmaid dresses I chose. Her daughter, who was in the wedding, "doesn't look good in emerald green." Obviously, I didn't change the dress color, but it was nonstop for the entire time up until the wedding. "Have you SEEN the color Emma chose?"… "That color will wash out the entire wedding party…or perhaps that's what you want?"… "Have you asked the photographer about the dress color? I'm concerned." It turned out fine. The photos are all framed in her house. Everyone looks great. Well, except for her daughter who actually *did* look pretty bad in emerald green. *–Emma, Nearly Contrite DIL*

Life Lesson from a Savvy DIL

Do you want a woman in your life who tells you what you want to hear or what she really thinks? It's possible she dreamed of her son's big day too, or maybe she's having trouble releasing control. Anticipate brutal honesty from your MIL and find a way for that to benefit you in the future! And don't gloat over the photos. *–Karolyn*

05

Pitter-Patter Coming Soon!

The lesson learned is to stand respectfully to the side when it comes to our daughters-in-law's pregnancies. This is their very special time with their partners **and** *with their mothers. The mother-in-law's job is negligible for the moment. But just you wait!*

Oh baby, I love your name

So, with grandchildren under my belt, I've learned to ask if the soon-to-be parents want input (they never do), and then to display passive exuberance when the topic comes up.

No surprise, we wanted to choose our own baby names. My husband and I spent many hours envisioning our future child and what we would call him or her. We would say a particular name over and over, to see if it wore well. When we finally got pregnant, we made the big old mistake of sharing our girl and boy names. My mother-in-law could not NOT voice her opinions. And would call with evidence she'd found of why the name was a bad idea. I was offended that she thought she had a vote. For our second baby, we shared nothing with her. –*Devon, Lesson Learned DIL*

Life Lesson from a Savvy DIL

Baby names are ultra-personal. That being said, people will always have opinions: The name is too popular, too old, too long or just plain ugly. Before saying anything, your mother-in-law should have stopped to consider how her comments might be received. Would you be offended and sad? Or would you brush them off because you love the name and don't care about her opinions? When she asks why you aren't sharing the name for the next baby, maybe gently tell her the truth. –*Megan*

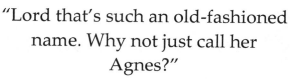

"Lord that's such an old-fashioned name. Why not just call her Agnes?"

–A mother-in-law who regretted that question for a long, long time

Enjoy the party, don't critique it

This story made me question what rule book Bonnie was reading, and more to the point, how long ago it was published.

My sorority sister's mom, Bonnie, offered to host a baby shower for me in the summer. Before the invitations had been mailed, I mentioned to my mother-in-law that it would be a late-morning gathering with a tea party theme. Her reaction was immediately negative, sort of appalled. So much so that I was a little panicky. What in the world had I said that caused her such alarm? Pretty quickly I got the answer. In her view, a tea party theme is meant for an afternoon event, not late-morning. I found out much later (thankfully) that she had phoned hostess Bonnie to suggest changing the time of day for the shower. Bonnie may be sweet, but she's no pushover. She did not change the plans, and the shower — teacups and all — was a big hit. *–Jody, Confused DIL*

 Life Lesson from a Savvy DIL

There's nothing to be done now. Given that you found out about this after your enjoyable baby shower, anything you do now will create unnecessary emotional drain and drag up history. Plus, the interaction happened between your MIL and Bonnie, so inserting yourself creates a drama triangle. Consider talking to your MIL proactively if a similar event is in your future — baby #2 perhaps? — sharing with her what behavior on her part will be the most helpful for and supportive of you. *–Shannon*

A secret isn't a secret if you tell your gaggle of friends

I can definitely relate to the power of knowing the kids were in the hospital (kudos to Janis for knowing how to track a cell phone). Just don't abuse that power!

My husband and I wanted the birth of our first child to be a private moment. Just him and me — no family, no visitors. We told the entire extended family about our decision. My mom was a bit sad, but she seemed to understand. My husband's mother Janis was incredulous and tried to get us to reconsider, which we did not. When I went into labor, we told no one. Our plan was to call them once the baby was born and settled in. Turns out, my mother-in-law had figured out how to track Jay's iPhone, so on the night I went into labor, she could see that he was at the hospital rather than at home. She then proceeded to call or text our family and her annoying gaggle of lady friends. We began to receive texts nonstop as we tried to settle in. This was two years ago, and I'm still not over being mad at her for it. –*Kathryn, Still-Mad DIL*

 **Life Lesson from a Savvy DIL**

This is fair. You made your wishes known and they were ignored! If she had just tracked his phone, or even tracked it and told immediate family, I might understand. This seems like too much excitement led to a lack of self-control. Has this type of behavior continued or was she apologetic? It may warrant a conversation so you can leave this water under the bridge. –*Karolyn*

Tip from a Pro MIL

Lips zipped

Unless expressly invited into the conversation, best to be the stoic and wise bystander when it comes to your daughter-in-law's pregnancy.

Me first! Me first!

Every time I think about this story, I wonder why the daddy-to-be (her son) didn't just politely decline.

My mother-in-law doesn't understand the concept of a gender reveal. In particular, the part about doing it in front of family and friends. She sees this as a private matter, not cause for a large get-together. Here's where it gets weird. She declined to attend our reveal party, insisting that we have a small luncheon later that week. This meant that the big reveal happened first, but everyone (including her other children) had to promise to stay off social media and to hide the baby's gender until the lunch, days later.
–Kerry, Twice Revealed DIL

 **Life Lesson from a Savvy DIL**

First, someone needs to explain to your MIL that the gender reveal is foremost for the parents-to-be. There really isn't any point in doing it twice. Rather than dwell on this instance, if you're intending to have more kids, maybe plan for how to handle this next time. –*Megan*

DIL Speak

Most Important Things Mothers-in-Law
Need to Know

1. *Listen. Really and truly listen.* We do value your life experience (even if sometimes it's there to tell us what NOT to do). We'd like to talk to you, run ideas by you, and speculate on the right or wrong way to approach a household matter, a recipe, a kid question. But if you interrupt before we've formed a thought or jump to a conclusion before we've had our say, we may not be back. Which is too bad, as that would be a missed opportunity for both of us.

2. *Do not pass judgment, at least not out loud.* Yours is a unique position. The only mother-in-law your child's partner will ever have. Hopefully. Don't blow it by interjecting judgment; be accepting, interested and passive. Even if it's an unnatural state, do not sit in judgment.

3. *Be helpful in your child's home.* You are NOT a house guest; you are family. Family help each other out. Family should not expect to have their plates cleared. Pitch in, and don't trade your help for expected gratuity (as in "thank you, that was so wonderful") at every instance.

4. *Embrace your child's partner.* Remember that you no longer have a relationship with just your child; you have a relationship with both of us. Of course, you have a sweet spot for your own child, but try to create a special relationship with your son/daughter-in-law too.

06

Grandparenting, Best Job on the Planet

It's the brass ring, these grandchildren. It's vaguely reminiscent of our own parenting days, but without the stress and strain of being on duty 24/7. The veteran grandparents knowingly tell you that there's nothing like it. And that it's wonderful. If that's true, you don't want to mess this up. And unlike parenting, we grandparents don't have the control. If you accept that there is a power curve lurking behind the mother-in-law journey, then believe that the balance here is soundly in the hands of your children and their partners.

It's not necessarily all fun and games, Grandma

I'm picturing the contrast here. Single mother-in-law doing the best she can versus the mighty mom-dad duo looking like Super Nannies.

My parents watch my son every Tuesday. My mother-in-law watches my son every Thursday. When I come home on Tuesdays, the house is humming with calm. A salad tossed and ready to serve. Spencer is bathed and settled in on the couch. Toys are put back where they belong. All is good. Thursdays? Not so much. There are toys everywhere. Spencer is still in his play clothes or, oddly, a diaper only. No salad, but plenty of dirty dishes. In both cases, my son is happy and safe, but the difference to me in terms of stress at the end of the workday is striking. All it would take is a nap-time cleanup to cleanse the chaos. I wonder what she does in those two hours? *–Tori, Under-Served DIL*

 **Life Lesson from a Savvy DIL**

Girl, don't bite the hand that feeds you! If this bothers you to the point of changing your daycare arrangements, fine. If not, ease up!! Everyone has their strengths and weaknesses, and of course you prefer the way your parents do things. Plus, there are two of them! Focus on the positives. Maybe praising her when she does things you like could get you more of what you want, instead of scoffing at what isn't ideal. *–Karolyn*

You Say, She Says. Who's Right?

~~~~~~

Appearance of favoritism

Daughter-in-Law: My mother-in-law favors her daughter's little girl Reagan. We all know that. But she makes it so obvious by how she displays photos of Reagan as compared to our son. It hurts my feelings, and I don't understand why she can't see that.

Mother-in-Law: I cannot possibly keep track of how many photos of the grandkids I frame or tape to the kitchen bulletin board. My daughter-in-law is way too sensitive about this. One time, she actually gave me a count: 5 pictures of Reagan, but only 3 of Will (her son).

~~~~~~

Birth room, by invitation only

Yikes, Joyce, let this one go. Some situations are simply off-limits.

My mother and my husband were at my sides for the birth of our first child. I wasn't sure how I would handle childbirth, and I wanted my mom there with me. I knew no matter what I blurted out or spewed, my mother would not hold it against me. My mother-in-law Joyce wasn't on the invite list. She was beside herself. This might be her last grandchild born (wrong). She has only sons, so in fairness, she couldn't quite grasp the mother-daughter thing. Even still, I wanted *my mom* there and not my mother-in-law. She turned that into a story, to be told year after year, that first hinted at and then later asserted my insensitivity. In one version, she offered that perhaps I was simply lacking in "maternal instinct." *–Jill, Birth Room Hostess DIL*

Life Lesson from a Savvy DIL

Hey, MILs: The process of childbirth is beyond stressful, for everyone, but especially the woman who is about to squeeze that watermelon out. Whether it is the first time or tenth time, that room and the visitors in it are up to her. I would argue the husband doesn't even really have a vote. If your DIL doesn't want you there, just let that be. It is not because she doesn't love you; it is because everyone has different opinions on who should hear them scream, hold their hand, or see their vagina. So back up and wait to hold that little thing when it's cleaned off and cuter anyway. *–Megan*

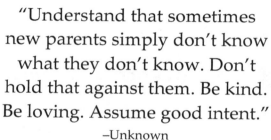

"Understand that sometimes new parents simply don't know what they don't know. Don't hold that against them. Be kind. Be loving. Assume good intent."

–Unknown

Shield your eyes, there's a baby in pink overalls

Momma may have figuratively tossed the baby out with the bath water on this one.

My mother-in-law has all sorts of rules about all sorts of unimportant things. One is about which stuffy outfit a baby in arms should wear to church. I learned this when we were visiting from out of town with our 6-month-old daughter who was dressed in pink corduroy overalls and pink booties. We met grandma at the church. She took one look at the outfit I had chosen, did one of her "tsk tsk" things, and after mass, herded us out the side door to avoid her fellow parishioners. She actually turned down a chance to show off what was then her only grandchild because the baby wasn't dressed to her standards. Again, the baby was not even able to crawl, nonetheless socialize. –*Fiona, Incredulous DIL*

 Life Lesson from a Savvy DIL

I can see how this bothers you, but I'd suggest taking another look at what is important to your MIL. Are these deal-breakers for you or can you let her do her thing? Before another event like this I'd ask what she would prefer your daughter to wear, or better yet, let her know she's free to send you outfits she'd love to see the baby in! –*Karolyn*

Which kind of grandmother will you be?

I can see both the working mom's dilemma and her mother-in-law's position too. P.S.: I'm fully jealous of Julia's extracurricular activities.

My advice on the grandmother thing is this. Figure out if they will be grandparents who occasionally babysit, or babysitters who are also grandparents. My MIL Julia wanted to be an everyday part of the kids' lives, so we arranged for her to come to the house every Friday. She chose the day. Before she retired, Julia worked outside of her home, so she knows that Friday is a workday just like the other four weekdays. Yet she routinely made plans for long weekends, starting on FRIDAY. Or, signed up for a workshop that requires travel on FRIDAY. I get it, she's not paid help, but she picked FRIDAY as her day. That put me in the impossible scenario of having to basically fire Nanna. –*Lauren, Hassled DIL*

 Life Lesson from a Savvy DIL

I hear you on the bait-and-switch pitch you got from your MIL, but I do think it takes time for grandparents to evolve into their roles, no different than it does for us becoming mothers. Grandparents like to envision "how they'll be," but won't truly know until life plays out. Once you start to identify this pattern with Nanna, take care of it immediately to spare yourself the stress of finding Friday childcare. Tell her you want to relieve her of her Friday duties to ensure she doesn't feel crippled by them. Whenever she wants to enjoy a Friday with her granddaughter, your nanny can play hooky! I realize this puts you out financially as you're paying for childcare, but it's a more reliable bet than socialite Nanna. –*Katie*

"If you have a lot of tension and you get a headache, do what it says on the aspirin bottle: 'Take two aspirin' and 'Keep away from children.'"

–Former First Lady Barbara Bush

I'm the mom, you're not

I feel like "your kid, your rules" needs to prevail here. But I'm a rule follower from way back when, so I'd actually prefer to be given instructions.

My husband's parents love to have any chance to watch our daughter, who is now 3 years old. From the start, when I left Gia in their care, I always provided a list of my expectations: nap time, snacks I provided, which walk is the best when going to the park, and so on. Evidently, my in-laws don't like to be told what to do. Invariably, when I get home, it's as if the list didn't exist. First hint? The snacks are still where I left them and the nap just didn't happen. My mother-in-law's response, "Well she's alive, isn't she?" *–Anna, Perplexed DIL*

Life Lesson from a Savvy DIL

There are two choices here:

Choice #1: Talk to your in-laws about why they choose not to follow your requests, share the impact it has on Gia (and you!) when she has a day without her usual routine (no nap!), and see if you can reach an agreement about them respecting your requests. You may need to be prepared to say what you will do differently if you cannot reach agreement.

Choice #2: Let it go. This really depends on how disruptive Gia's "re-entry" is to your immediate family after time with her Grand Ps. Assuming there's no long-term collateral damage, perhaps let your in-laws form an independent relationship with your kids, who will benefit from lots of grandparent time in their lives. This brings life-long value, which perhaps outweighs your need for structure. *–Shannon*

Gift-giving in hyperdrive

This MIL could be my own mother, so I can say from first-hand experience that we never broached the topic. I would have hurt her feelings forever.

We have one child, and she is my in-laws' first grandchild. They are very generous in general, but the introduction of a grandbaby has put their gift-buying into hyperdrive. Of course, some of the gifts are wanted and welcome, but some are not. It's impossible to say "no thank you," so now I literally have a cabinet in our garage filled with extra gifts, from tens of zip-up sleepers to children's furniture. And my in-laws either haven't noticed the "missing" gifts or they *have* noticed but for some reason aren't asking. I know that we should be cautiously honest with them about this, but my husband's take is that would make the situation considerably worse. Or, as he says, "It won't end well…for you." –*Maria, Lips Zipped DIL*

 Life Lesson from a Savvy DIL

Your husband is probably right. He may know that any comments on the topic will be blamed on you, the daughter-in-law. Whether or not it's historically accurate, their son probably "always appreciated [their] generosity." So in their minds, you must be the reason for the change.

I suggest that you still have the honest conversation, and try to do so in the nicest way possible. Although I'm not sure I would have it in me. I would probably let that crap pile up until "it doesn't fit her anymore…." Then donate it. –*KC*

Tip from a Pro MIL

Give from your heart, then let it go

Give gifts to your grandchildren from your heart, and don't be offended or put off if the gifts aren't all received in the same fashion. One of my daughters-in-law tucks away the baby blankets that I knit, wanting to hold onto the handmade "treasures." Another daughter-in-law uses them every day, until they are ragged with loving care. Another blanket, I've never seen or heard of since it was mailed — might be in Goodwill for all I know. Am I offended? No. Why should I care? It gave me pleasure to give them.

You say Nonna, I say Grannie

Here's what I say. Who cares what they call me? Except perhaps if it was "Mrs. Dunne."

My mother-in-law wants my children (not born yet) to call her by a specific name. This is how she presented that instruction: "I am not going to be called Gammie, or Grammy or Grandma. I'm not ready to be seen as old enough to be a grandmother." It was all I could do to not point out the obvious, that if you ARE a grandmother, YOU are old enough to be seen as one. She let us know that she would allow to be referred to as "Nonna" or "Mimi." Her name is Suzanne, so neither of those make any particular sense. Unless something unusual happens, my children will be Suzanne's first grandchildren, so as my luck would have it, I am in the position to influence the situation. My plan is to start referring to her over and over as "Grannie Suzanne" and see how that plays out. I realize this is childish, but I believe I should have the control, Grannie. *–Andrea, Self-Aware DIL*

 Life Lesson from a Savvy DIL

I wanted my kids to call my mother "Sammy." (Long story why.) Anyway, she rejected it. So my sister and I came up with something she hated more: "Gam Gam." In the end, we all lost. My daughter changed "Gam Gam" into "Gammy." This is not a battle worth fighting. Let the woman be called whatever she wants. Maybe your kid will magically change Nonna into something else entirely all on her own, and you'll get the last laugh. *–KC*

Tip from a Pro MIL

Love equally

It's OK, and to be expected, that you will have different relationships with each of your grandchildren. Unless you are all living in the same house or in the same community, proximity means that you get to know some more than others. The grandkids don't really notice the differences between the relationships, unless their "well-meaning" parents start that conversation. But it's all-important to love them equally. I give the same gifts at Christmas. I knit a blanket for each new baby. My fridge has school photos of every child.

Those were MY curly locks to shear

Here's a mother-in-law who apparently doesn't mind poking a sleeping momma bear.

When my son was about 6 months old, we came to stay with my mother-in-law for a long weekend. To give us some alone time, she sent us off with her credit card and instructions to enjoy a leisurely lunch at the beach. While we were enjoying our lunch, marveling at the unexpected gesture, my mother-in-law took Jacob to the barber because his baby locks "made him look like a little girl." Yep, that was his first haircut, just he and grandma. No photo was taken, no lock of hair saved, no memory for us. –*Lila, Astounded DIL*

 Life Lesson from a Savvy DIL

WHOA. *Not OK.* Astounded is an understatement. I'd use this as an immediate opportunity to set boundaries regarding milestones: "Thank you so much for treating us to a beach getaway; what a treat! While we're so grateful, we were definitely disappointed to miss Jacob's first haircut — a big milestone for us, *as his parents.* Next time you're thinking about doing a 'first' with him, can you run it by us before? We may want to join or have something planned to celebrate." –*Katie*

DIL Speak

Drive-by Commentary Not Spoken Here

I know there's room for debate on this one, but I'm learning that less is better when it comes to offering advice to tired, stressed young parents. Also, I like the idea of a quote-of-the-month calendar.

I think my mother-in-law either has absolutely no emotional intelligence, or she truly does not care. She makes "drive-by" comments about basically everything, but as a grandmother and mother-in-law, she's particularly prolific. I've been saving up her comments so I can make a quote-of-the-month calendar. A few of the more choice ones:

> "I don't think babies can sleep with those bright colors" (in the newly decorated nursery).

> "You indulge them entirely — nothing left for me to do. Why would I bother trying?"

> "Funny. You're worrying about walking at the time I was working on potty training."

> "There's a better way to hold a newborn. Well maybe not better. Safer."

> "If they can hold their own bottle, they can hold a sippy cup."

> "Swaddling? Looks more like a baby straitjacket. Is that safe?"

The Thing About Facebook

Many of our children cut their social media teeth on Facebook, and then went on to discard it for other platforms like Instagram, Twitter and who knows what else. Meanwhile, we're still back rather enjoying Facebook. Like with all things to do with being an in-law, when using Facebook, just don't overshare.

Is this your song to sing?

Sometimes we just need to be forgiven for our innocent exuberance.

My future mother-in-law sends out a holiday photo collage card every year. Of course, because it is *her* card, she has full control of the contents. I understand that. We got engaged over Thanksgiving and told my parents first on Thanksgiving Day, then flew to see my fiancé's parents to tell them. They were also thrilled and took photos of us with champagne flutes in hand. Evidently, during our flight home, my future MIL posted the flute photo on her Facebook page, meaning she announced our engagement to extended family and mutual friends for us. We had planned to tell our friends on our own time. Oh well. –*Kaitlynne, Graciously Annoyed DIL*

 Life Lesson from a Savvy DIL

This sounds like an innocent mistake. The good news is your in-laws are thrilled for you to join their family. Now that you know she's an eager poster, make it clear when you do not want something shared on Facebook or when you'd like to be the first to share. This will help her learn to be more sensitive and aware while navigating the intersecting worlds of family and social media. –*Shannon*

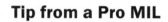

Tip from a Pro MIL

Facebook foibles

My son is in the service and was deployed. My daughter-in-law called to say that she had the results of the sonogram and that baby #2 was a boy. I was so excited. That afternoon, I went on Facebook and commented that I would be looking for blue yarn in time for the next baby blanket. I had assumed she had told my son already, but as it turns out, she had not. She was furious.

Back away from the post

My first reaction was an eye roll on this story. But given KC's comment below, I'm a believer.

The problem is not that my mother-in-law posted a photo of our twins on Facebook. My issue is that, unknown to me, she has no privacy restrictions, so the photo was seen by Lord-who-knows. The photo featured grandma standing in her driveway with my little darlings. The problem was that it included views of her street number and her car license plate (number and name of local car dealer) for all to zoom in and see. It was like a scene from *Criminal Minds*. She thinks I'm overreacting. Probably am. –*Marta, Under-Reacting DIL*

 Life Lesson from a Savvy DIL

If your MIL doesn't realize what she has done, you may still have to approach it kindly. But man, I would lose it, Marta. Here's why. With just her name, a basic understanding of her location within the country, and the address numbers, I could find out her full address, phone number and close relatives (and their addresses) within 5 minutes using just Google. There are dangerous people out there (OK, full disclosure I am also in the law enforcement field). Scary, but true. You do not want a random person knowing exactly where to find your MIL or your children. –*KC*

Tip from a Pro MIL

Think before you post

As my daughter-in-law recently explained to me: "Facebook is a public forum, woman." I have learned to never *ever* leave messages like these:

> "Hope you two work things out."

> "Always great to see you…do I hear wedding bells?"

> "Sooo happy! Let me know when you make the big announcement."

> "Looks like it's time for a threesome!" (I was referring to a new baby, which itself would have been a bad idea.)

Ask yourself, how might this backfire?

Wouldn't you just love to be a fly on the wall for the mother-son conversation?

My boyfriend's mother doesn't get it. At all. She can't grasp the concept that posting a comment on one's FB is NOT the same as relaying a private message. There have been several show-stopping incidents. My personal favorite being when her son and I had been dating for a couple of months. Karen posted a comment on my FB, "Please marry my son. You are the first girl he introduced us to that we like." While I appreciate the intended compliment, it became a big-time source of embarrassment when my hundreds of FB friends started commenting in turn. *—Elena, Bemused DIL*

 **Life Lesson from a Savvy DIL**

This one is tough because, like it or not, our parents' generation will NOT meet our expectations on social media. The sooner you accept that, the better. However, I think an attempt at damage control is worth your while. (1) Delete any of her comments on your page or ask your boyfriend to on his; spare yourself the embarrassment and don't worry that it may confuse her. (2) Explain to her directly that while those comments are appreciated, they can be seen by everyone, so you often delete people's comments to avoid further swirl personally or professionally. And like it or not, it's time to accept the cringe-worthy moments that come with social media and our parents. *—Katie*

08

Evil Twins: Finding Fault and Predicting Failure

With age comes wisdom, and with wisdom comes knowledge. From there it can be a slippery slope to judgment and criticism. Finding fault and predicting failure is unwelcome in any situation, but young couples and young parents have absolutely no patience for such things. Many of their stories seem impossibly extreme — as in, who in their right mind would say or do that? But apparently many did. Cautionary tales.

Good money for a good cause

Sticks and stones...but words will never hurt. Except when they do.

My 5-year-old daughter has a crazy set of teeth. They seriously go every which way. We for sure know she has years of orthodontics in her future. To me, there's nothing cuter than when she gives us a gigantic smile with her freckles and crooked teeth on display. We dressed her in her favorite frilly party dress, and got a portrait taken of her at the mall. I hung it in the front hall at home, along with a bunch of other fave photos. The next time the in-laws were over, my mother-in-law did a double take on the new photo, and said loudly, "You paid good money for that?" *–Bella, Pleasure Spender DIL*

 Life Lesson from a Savvy DIL

Stand your ground on this! When your MIL said, "You paid good money for that?" I would have responded with pride, "I did! And I love it! Why do you ask?" Orthodontics needed or not, your daughter is beautiful just the way she is, and that should be celebrated. Remember, you don't need your MIL to agree with you, just to hold her tongue in your home. ;) *–Katie*

When the golden rule doesn't rule

You know it's bad when the son is calling out his own mother.

When it came time for our baby shower, my wife's family and friends planned the first shower. They reserved space in their family's favorite Indian restaurant — one that served from a long buffet bar. I had explained to my mom over and over that Kyra's family entertained in their own traditions and that Mom needed to be a gracious guest. I was asking too much of her, which I kind of knew would be the case. She spent the entire two hours rolling her eyes, tsk tsk-ing as she walked along the buffet, with heavy sighs throughout. When I pulled her aside to insist that she stop, her response was, "What? I haven't said a word about this tacky party." It's like she cannot help herself. *–Kevin, Valiant SIL*

Life Lesson from a Savvy DIL

There's nothing to say about this behavior. There's no fixing it. This is a mother-in-law who seems not to care about her daughter-in-law or her own son — and deeply believes she can do no wrong. There is no remedy. You can call her out, she will be defensive. You can have a nice, calm conversation and she might agree she shouldn't have done that, but will do it again, the same way, at the baby shower. Over time, she will make herself the villain without anyone else pointing it out. *–KC*

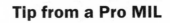

Tip from a Pro MIL

Avoid remembering when

"When I was your age…" Unless that sentence ends with admission of insecurity or mistakes made, stop talking.

Pollyanna you're not

Sometimes you need to land on the side of logic, not fear-mongering.

My daughter was in a nasty snowboarding accident and had to have fairly significant surgery to repair torn ligaments and broken bones in her knee, wrist and ankle. She was young enough (14 years) and her recovery prolonged enough (4 weeks) that we needed daytime care beyond what my wife and I could extract from our available vacation time at our jobs. My bachelor brother offered to stay with us for one of the weeks, holding down the fort and being there when the visiting nurse and physical therapists came to the house. My mother-in-law's reaction? "Be careful with that. You know that young girls can get attached to their caretakers — it's called the Stockholm Syndrome. You could be putting your brother in a delicate situation." *–Kelsey, Shocked DIL*

 **Life Lesson from a Savvy DIL**

Nope. Gross. No words. *–Megan*

Let's call her Cruella

For this mother-in-law, the concept of "loving grandma" was somehow lost along the way.

My mother-in-law is mean. Picture a tall, gaunt woman with jet black hair and a shock of white in front. You know, Cruella de Vil. There's no changing her, so I have no particular advice to give — only plenty of stories to share. One in particular stands out. We were out for a relaxing lunch. As if recalling a fond memory, she said, "Watching your son with the other kids at Christmas dinner, it's clear that he really stands out." I'm thinking it's because he's 6 foot with a great smile and gigantic blue eyes. But then she follows with, "Because he didn't go to college like everybody else did."
–Melanie, No Words DIL

 Life Lesson from a Savvy DIL

Jeeze! At least she's consistent. Take what she says with a grain of salt, or steer clear. –*Karolyn*

Like a boxer, she goes for the KO

This story calls to mind Disney's Thumper. "If you can't say something nice..."

After two years of sporadic attendance at the local community college, my 19-year-old son talked to us about working for a winter in a Colorado ski resort. He would live in dormitory-style housing, work 40 hours a week or more for minimum wage, and spend the rest of his time snowboarding and drinking beer. We were all for it — he was going to be OUT OF THE HOUSE, and probably learning some life lessons about hard work and how far minimum wage can take you. At our Thanksgiving dinner table, in response to his grandmother's question about how school was going, Cole brightened up and started to explain that he was going to move to Colorado to work at a ski resort. At least I think he got that far before my mother-in-law pounced on him. Her immediate reaction was, "And who is going to pay for THAT pipe dream? Don't answer. We all know your parents will be funding this just like they always do."
–*Jesse, Momma Bear DIL*

 Life Lesson from a Savvy DIL

Bold move by your MIL, Jesse. Bold! She clearly took a shot, but I wouldn't entertain this beyond a quick pivot. Whether or not you are funding this isn't her business and isn't the point of the conversation. Shut...Her...Down. "We haven't nailed down the financing on this yet, but it looks like you clearly have an opinion on that, [MIL]! Back to the point of the conversation, we're really excited for Cole's new plans. Tell everyone about the apartment you found, Cole!" Moving on... –*Katie*

Tip from a Pro MIL

Hold that thought

If you have concerns, don't voice them. You raised your children, so trust them to make good choices.

Your history is not her future

I'm no doctor, but I'm confident we have no business drawing conclusions about someone else's pregnancy.

As she told it, my mother-in-law had been depressed during each of her four pregnancies and in the four or five months following each birth. Given she had four children in five years, I calculate that she was pretty much depressed for five years straight. So when I was pregnant with our first baby, she predicted that I would be a mess during the pregnancy, which I wasn't. Then when she came to stay with us after the baby was born, she constantly recalled her own post-delivery woes. If I was testy or even sighed out loud, she was almost happy — "See, you have the depression, too." Truthfully, she could have *made* me depressed. –Lindsay, "I'm Good" DIL

Life Lesson from a Savvy DIL

First, what were you thinking letting your mother-in-law stay with you after the baby was born? There's a rule about messing with a postpartum mom. Unsolicited input — especially negative — on pregnancy or mental/emotional state is never welcome. –KC

No, you aren't "just wondering"

I say small talk, you say super annoying. Just wondering.

My mother-in-law is generally very nice, and passive to the point of being submissive. There is one really odd exception to this: my kitchen. Here's an example. We have this big clock on the wall. It broke a while back so now it's essentially wallpaper. Every visit, my mother-in-law asks, "When are you going to get that clock fixed?" Similarly, "You need more cabinets. I can't find anything when I'm here." Or, "Why aren't the utensils next to the dishwasher?" What really annoys me is that she *always* starts
the question with "Hadley, dear..." and ends with, "I'm just wondering." My husband thinks I'm being ridiculous ("Mom doesn't mean anything by that.") but it makes me crazy. –*Hadley, Prickly DIL*

 **Life Lesson from a Savvy DIL**

I'm on your side on this one, Hadley. Totally annoying, and it's hard to say if it's conscious or unconscious behavior. Maybe as a submissive woman, in her life her kitchen was the only domain she controlled? Either way, a chat with your MIL is in order. Share with her your desire for her to visit and be a part of your family. Let her know you're curious about her intent in making these comments (be prepared to really listen to her response). See if you can reach an agreement about her not doing this going forward! –*Shannon*

"My mother-in-law's favorite expression is 'You need to…' I've heard it so many times, it's now like fingernails on a chalkboard."

–Unknown

09

Say What You Mean, Mean What You Say

In a conversation when one side speaks in loose generalities, while the other side interprets it all literally, there's going to be disconnect. In other words, say what you mean and mean what you say. Easier said than done it seems.

No take-backs on generous offers

She had me at "Boulder farmhouse."

My fiancé's parents offered to host our wedding. The house was great. A Boulder farmhouse. In the months ahead of the wedding, my in-laws remodeled the guest bathroom and re-landscaped the backyard. They had a pergola built. They were over the top in buying and preparing for the event. It looked amazing and was the talk of the wedding. Years later, there would be the occasional comment about extra dollars they "had to" spend on the wedding. Speculation that they would never "get back" the full amount of money and time put into the farmhouse property for the wedding. This really hurt my feelings. Why didn't she say so at the time? We liked the house and grounds as they were. *–Abby, Stung DIL*

 Life Lesson from a Savvy DIL

Toughie. Hosting something always comes with the stress of people judging the host. When your in-laws opened up their home to people for a wedding, they did so because they wanted to. That said, I personally think a few jokes here and there are OK. Maybe you need to lighten up a bit. But be cautious and watch for the boiling-over point! In the end, your in-laws have a better-looking house, and they did a very nice thing for you! *–Megan*

You Say, She Says. Who's Right?

∿∿∿

Ride sharing

Daughter-in-law: My mother-in-law is a long-time divorcee who lives independently, but does not drive (she wisely turned in her license a few years back). She travels the world with hiking clubs and other senior-oriented clubs. Yet she isn't comfortable riding in an Uber or Lyft alone. Because we live in the same general area, she expects one of us to take her and pick her up from the airport, which is 30 minutes away — longer if during the commute hours. It feels like she is taking advantage of us.

Mother-in-law: My kids think it's "no big deal" to order up a complete stranger to pick me up from the airport and drop me at my house. The whole concept makes me uncomfortable, so I have asked for my kids' help. You would think they'd want me safe and unafraid, but mostly they act like I'm being trivial and taking advantage of them.

∿∿∿

Tip from a Pro MIL

Sometimes you just gotta go for it

My daughter-in-law likes things "just so." She is a
wonderful homemaker, and everything has its place. She
prides herself, rightfully so, on her organizational skills.
Her mom and I were both at the house helping with the
grandkids while Lara was at work. While looking for tea
bags, I accidentally knocked over a container of sugar in
her Lazy Susan cupboard. I started to clean it up and
then realized that all the shelves in the Lazy Susan could
use a dose of dusting and, in some cases, deep cleaning.
My daughter-in-law's mother said, "Oh no, do NOT
fiddle with her Lazy Susan. If I did that, she would
throw a fit." I decided that this was easy territory for a
mother-in-law. Lara knows that I am not judgmental,
that I only want to help her. So I cleaned it up — no
more sugar tossed round, all lids on tight. Did she
appreciate the effort? I don't know. I never asked nor did
I expect her to thank me.

Find your shared language

I love this story. They each found their lanes, and it worked out oh so well.

I really never learned to cook. I have three go-to recipes, all of which require less than 5 different ingredients and can be made in about 30 minutes. My mother-in-law, however, is well known for being an amazing cook. So I asked her for some recipes that my husband might enjoy. She was gracious and enthusiastic — sending me photocopies from her own recipe card catalog and from magazines she enjoyed. Not only was it good information to have, but it also brought us closer together because it was a shared language where we could agree on our respective jobs — she was the expert and I was the newcomer. Now, 30 years later, my own children are using Oma's hand-me-down recipes in their homes. *–Nicole, Happy Co-Pilot DIL*

 Life Lesson from a Savvy DIL

Love this! You opened the door for Oma to weigh in and coach you in a certain area, subtly illustrating that there are no boundaries when it comes to the kitchen. Let her be the expert, and you the student. I think regardless of how strong a MIL-DIL relationship is, and even if we don't take much interest in a particular topic, this is a GREAT example of how to allow for growth in a relationship. Ask your MIL for help in an area you know she excels in, or at least thinks she does. Stroke her ego; let her be the hero! While there is no competition here, you can essentially let her win. *–Katie*

10

Passing the Baton of Control

In this new world, respecting boundaries and letting go of the need to control is necessary and, apparently, tough to do for many of us. Even so, it's all-important to find the right balance between, figuratively speaking, winning the skirmishes while over time, losing the war. This wrestle between mothers and their daughters-in-law was perhaps the strongest theme among all of the young women I interviewed. They see this chapter as their time, just as we did a generation ago.

You thought this was clever. Really?

Sandra seems out of line, but then again, she had the power and yielded it with zeal.

My mother-in-law doesn't agree with my parenting style. She thinks I am too strict and controlling. I discount her point of view. Her other grandchildren — her daughter's children who live with her — are ill-behaved. When she is watching my kids, she subverts my position in order to ease the rules for my kids.

I have a rule that there is no jumping on beds or couches. My mother-in-law thinks "that's a shame." She was babysitting my 5-year-old, and when I came home, all of the couch cushions were on the floor lined up end to end. My son explained that Grandma and he were playing indoor hopscotch on the couch cushions. When I confronted my mother-in-law, her response was, "You said no jumping on THE COUCH...we were on the floor." That was the last time she babysat. – *Sandra, Passively Aggressive DIL*

Life Lesson from a Savvy DIL

Yikes, that's pretty passive-aggressive. You have two choices in my opinion. Look the other way and let your children and their grandmother enjoy each other and have fun games and "secrets." Or, limit their time with her unless she can adhere to your rules. What's more important to you? Look at the bigger picture mama. *–Karolyn*

"My mother-in-law's mantra is
'Blood is thicker than water,' which
she demonstrates in so many ways.
Once I understood that, it was
GAME ON lady."

–Unknown

A "highly motivated" opportunity to look foolish

This story is so outlandish that it can only be true. No making this up.

We had made an offer pending on a townhouse — our first home together. My mother-in-law was convinced we were paying too much for a property that needed substantial work. So she called the seller's realtor, presenting herself as an interested party and "highly motivated" buyer who wanted to see the inspection reports. The problem was her phone had caller ID, and our last name is distinct. The seller's realtor called our realtor, who called us. We then called Jackie (my mother-in-law) who was unapologetic. "I was just trying to help you!!!!" By the way, her big plan was to detect foundation or electrical problems significant enough to give us reason to ask for a reduced sales price. Never mind that we had already reviewed the same reports and found no problems. *–Rachel, Dumbfounded DIL*

 **Life Lesson from a Savvy DIL**

Seriously?! Dear MIL Jackie: Let the professionals do their jobs. This isn't just a MIL lesson, it's a life lesson. Don't be the person who calls the plumber and hovers over him the whole time, telling him where the leak is and which wrench to use. A realtor's job is to find the right house, for the best price, and no major issues. You are not their realtor. And, in a larger sense, don't be your son's protector. Not only does he not need one, he does not want one. So it's time to allow him to be an adult and watch how amazing that is! He is raised. You did it. *–Megan*

"My mother-in-law cannot help but intervene when my wife and I are discussing even the most mundane issues. 'Oh, just let him…' She always takes my side, and that does NOT help me. I'm having to basically negotiate both sides – I can't win. Someone's always upset."

–Unknown

Let. It. Go.

Short but not-so-sweet, Kimberly's story reflects the prevalent theme of control among the voices of her fellow DILs.

My mother-in-law has controlled everything all her adult life: her husband, her siblings, her friends and her children. She simply must be the center of attention. It's ingrained in who she is. When she isn't in charge, when it's not all about her, she doesn't want to participate. Try as she might, there really wasn't any way for her to control my pregnancy. And it certainly wasn't all about her. When we scheduled the ultrasound where we could learn the baby's gender, we invited her, but she declined. Same for the birth. Her loss. *—Kimberly, "I tried" DIL*

Life Lesson from a Savvy DIL

I agree with Kimberly. She tried to be inclusive (so props to her), but her mother-in-law apparently couldn't see the offer for what it was — an opportunity to be part of something rather than in control of it. *—KC*

"I have a great mother-in-law. She respects our boundaries and doesn't pry. She never asked 'when?' for babies. I can go to her for any advice. She is not judgmental. She doesn't feel she has license to judge or interfere."

–Unknown

Know when to say no

Hey Jason, thanks but no thanks. We MILs like going on your family vacations.

My wife and I invite my mother-in-law to every major event and, since she has been widowed, our family vacations. We do this out of both want and a sense of obligation — she does so much for us. But sometimes, it would be nice if she declined to attend. Only every so often, so we can have our own family time without Grandma. *–Jason, Wistful SIL*

 Life Lesson from a Savvy DIL

Nah Jason, this one is on you and your wife (her daughter). You don't get to make yourself feel better by inviting her, but then get disappointed that she accepts. If you don't want her there, don't invite her and suffer the guilt pangs. We invite my mom to everything, including vacations as well, but we almost always arrive earlier or stay later so we get family time too. *–KC*

Your rules, my kids

I'll give Eli's mom a break here. Clearly she's never seen a vegetarian up close.

I am engaged to a great guy, from a great family. Eli's mom is a bit buttoned down for my tastes, but she has always done her best to make me feel welcomed and liked.

She loves to entertain, and they entertain a lot. She insists on doing all of the cooking herself. The problem is that I am a confirmed vegetarian. I eat NO meats of any kind. Eli's mom just doesn't seem to grasp what this REALLY means. There have been meals where there was literally nothing I could eat. The green salad (with bacon bits) and the cheese (and pancetta) quiche don't work for me. Once she said, "It's close enough." I can't offer to help by bringing an additional dish because that's against her rules. I have subtly explained that I can't eat bacon or pancetta. Her response was, "can't or won't?"

I can see exactly how this is going to play out. I intend to raise our children as vegetarians, and if I can't trust their future grandmother to respect my wishes, I will not be leaving my kids under her care. No weekend sleepovers at Grandma's. –*Isla, Battle Lines Drawn DIL*

 Life Lesson from a Savvy DIL

Does this happen every time you eat at her house or just for these big parties? It's clearly unthoughtful, so I wonder why she won't accommodate you. Take a step back and try to figure out what it is. Could your dietary choices make her question her own, or is she just a big believer in doing things the way they've always been done? Worry about the children later; for now, help your MIL understand why this is so important to you. –*Karolyn*

Who really needs two moms?

This is another common theme I heard. Moms, be moms first — to your actual children.

My mother talks to my mother-in-law frequently, and it's weird. They talk about me, and they talk about my husband. They talk about our children. Then my mother reports to me what they have concluded. If it was as simple as talking about a specific thing, like comparing notes on a birthday gift to be sure they aren't duplicating, that would be fine. But they talk about BIG things, like whether we are spoiling our 3-year-old who is enrolled in a local daycare program. I don't think my mother-in-law realizes that I get a full report from my mom, so I'm finding myself irritated with my mother-in-law. Also, I don't like that my own relationship with my "actual" mother is changing now that there is a "second" mom in the equation. I know this sounds crazy, if not fully selfish, but I think I would prefer if they weren't trying to be friends. –*Meredith, Actual Daughter + DIL*

Life Lesson from a Savvy DIL

What an interesting scenario! While I understand your issue, I think it's very special that they've connected and become friends — evidence of an investment in your marriage and family. I do think, however, your mom shouldn't be sharing their private "conclusions" and "theories" with you. My advice: Let their friendship flourish, but tell your mom you don't want her to share these discussions with you. That should be kept private between the two of them, and it's best you not let it tarnish your relationship with your MIL. If she has concerns about an issue, she can come to you directly. –*Katie*

Mind your manners

I can so see myself doing something like this, but maybe best to wield the remote control only in our own homes.

Maggie's christening was the same Saturday as a USC football game. My husband Lance is a "Trojan," and for him and his friends, it doesn't really matter who they are playing. Every game is cause to gather around the biggest flat-screen TV available. We had come back from the christening to our 900-square-foot house for brunch. The gals — moms, aunts and grandmas — assembled in our tiny kitchen. Maggie was in her bassinette napping after her big day. The guys — dads, brother, uncles — grabbed cold beers and collected in the living/family room where our TV was located. As the game progressed, the roar from the living room increased. The cheers and the roars were hard to talk over. At one point — clearly offended that her granddaughter's big day was being overcome by football — my mother-in-law walked in, grabbed the remote and turned the TV off. I was impressed she knew how.

I actually felt sorry for her when Lance, who did not find it amusing, made his feelings known loud and clear. –*Heather, Happily Sidelined DIL*

 Life Lesson from a Savvy DIL

Your MIL isn't wrong in her intentions. More about her execution. Which could probably be said about *most* bad mother-in-law stories. I bet she told her own kids to use their words before acting out. She clearly should have asked that they keep it down first. But if she truly just wanted her granddaughter's day to be special, then you can't fault her *too* much. As for Lance, he probably didn't handle it well either. But hey, she raised him. –*KC*

Buddy system not recommended

A theme that bears repeating, with a twist: Daughter, be daughters first.

My mother was essentially jealous of my mother-in-law. Early on, I planned a mother-daughter day for the three of us. Disaster. First, my mom and my mother-in-law don't share the same food or shopping preferences. My mom is a vegetarian; my mother-in-law loves food trucks. My mom is a Nordstrom gal; my mother-in-law is a power Target shopper. The list goes on and on. Second, it became this weird competition for my attention. I realized later that I actually was favoring my mother-in-law, assuming my own mom would understand. Well, turns out my mom has a few insecurities of her own, and due to my "kowtowing" as she called it, I had hurt my mom's feelings. Like I said, it was a disaster. *–Becky, Kowtower DIL*

 Life Lesson from a Savvy DIL

My advice is for Becky's mom. Maybe this is a good set up for the moms to have a lunch date alone. You will most likely not become best friends with each other, but you two can certainly create a relationship independent of your respective daughter and daughter-in-law. It gives you two a chance to create a bond, if only a small one, that allows your daughter to relax and not try to make it work by herself. *–Megan*

Grandma's rules. Who rules?

Kudos to Sangeeta, who knows when to fold up her tent.

Negotiating rules — ours versus hers — can be exhausting. But we try to do so. We explain to my mother-in-law the rationale for "our rules" so we can hear first-hand how she plans to bend if not ignore our rules. For example, we say no sweets until year 2. She says, "Hope you don't mind, but I gave the baby some ice cream." I came to realize that this was less about challenging our rules for the sake of doing so, and mostly about loving indulgence and giving our kids, her grandchildren, a different experience and perspective. Borrowing from the corporate world, she was providing the children inclusiveness AND diversity! –*Sangeeta, Resigned DIL*

Life Lesson from a Savvy DIL

Your approach may not work for everyone, but kudos to you, Sangeeta. You came around to realize this is a losing battle with grandparents. They waited this long to NOT have rules with their grandchildren; how dare you rob them of this pleasure! Let your MIL break the rules, bend them, and outright ignore them, assuming your child's safety is never compromised. This is part of their job description, and sounds like she excels in the role! –*Katie*

Not your son's personal assistant

To have or not have birthday cards, that is the question here. Come on Brittany, give your clueless hubby a break!

My issue with my mother-in-law is that somehow she has come to believe that it is MY job to remember my husband's family birthdays. First, he has a huge family. But even if it was a small number, how is that my responsibility? She let me know this "rule" after David missed a key birthday. Maybe I would have stepped in to help my clueless husband, but after being read the riot act by his mom, I now actively refuse to help out at all. Hope you're happy, Elizabeth. *–Brittany, Not My Job DIL*

 Life Lesson from a Savvy DIL

Antiquated. Our generation doesn't keep address books or a rolodex of human information. We get notified about these things from social media. We have a group text where my parents remind us of birthdays in the family. If Brittany's MIL cares that her son texts his second-cousin, twice-removed, *she* needs to remind him. *–Megan*

Tip from a Pro MIL

Stay in your lane

When it comes to your son or daughter's life with their partner and children, you don't own that relationship. Nor should you. Take yourself out of their relationship. It's *their* relationship.

Hey buttinsky, butt out

This story reminds me to curb my appetite for being the inspector general of the kids' households.

My mother-in-law is a career "buttinsky." She is constantly giving me suggestions, which to me feel like one criticism after the other. The toilet paper roll should go over, not under. The forks and knives should never be placed in the dishwasher with their sharp points facing up. Denim is not appropriate for church. A baby with a pacifier means the baby will need braces. The spices can't be stored above the stovetop. Never ever let a baby cry more than 7 minutes. And on and on. And by the way, she expresses all of this in the form of innocent questions: Do you think it's wise...? Did you know that...?

I wish she would just keep her opinions to herself. I dread her visits. I once very nicely asked her if she could maybe think twice on some of her pronouncements. Her response was, "It's my responsibility to give advice to my children, no matter that they don't still live under my roof." *–Ami, Under Siege DIL*

 **Life Lesson from a Savvy DIL**

Aargh! Ami, your MIL sounds like a passive-aggressive nightmare. Confront this head-on. You can't effectively fight passive-aggressive behavior with more of the same. Let her know that advice disguised in the form of questions is unwelcome. Make a very specific request about how her behavior needs to change, sharing clearly how you'll choose to respond if she's unable to agree. Let her know you want her to be a part of your family, which is not the same thing as endlessly offering advice. Try enrolling your husband in this plan and/or asking him to lead the discussion. *–Shannon*

Tip from a Pro MIL

Whose rules rule?

If you take the "My House, My Rules" approach, then you need to respect that same position in your son or daughter's home.

MIL Speak

10 Killer MIL Phrases to Avoid

1. In my day…

2. You aren't actually going to…

3. What kind of name is…

4. If you had only thought to…

5. How much weight have you gained since…

6. Well, it's not what I expected, but…

7. How much did you pay for…

8. It's not *entirely* your fault…

9. You're not serious…

10. I make it a rule that…

11

Just Love Them

Daughters-in-law want to be respected and allowed to make their own choices, and even mistakes. But you know what? They also want to be loved by their mothers-in-law. Tales from DILs of poor relationships abound, but the stories here show us what's possible by way of the admiration and love described.

Starting with like, ending with love

At first, I thought this story was just about tough love from a tough mom, but it turned out to be so much more.

My mother was a famous critic. Fortunately, she was also pretty funny, and very loving toward her children, but nonetheless, if there was a flaw, she would not only find it but also discuss it over and over. She'd pull on that thread until the sweater finally unraveled. My expectations of my husband's mother were therefore pretty low. I expected judgment, but quietly hoped for better. What a surprise to find out that she liked me from Day 1, and loved me absolutely thereafter. She embodied "you make my son happy, so therefore I love you, too." I never told her how much that meant to me, but I suspect she knew. *–Jennifer, Lucky with Love DIL*

 Life Lesson from a Savvy DIL

This is beautiful to hear. What a gift she's given you to support and love you from Day 1. Tell her how grateful you are for her, and let it be a reminder for when you become a MIL one day! *–Katie*

Your son-in-law is watching too

I sincerely doubt that David was her favorite, but cute that he thinks so.

I really think my mother-in-law liked me best! It was like I was king for the day whenever my wife and I visited her parents. What was my favorite dinner? Would I like a second glass of wine? Would I prefer a different TV show? She didn't have any sons, so I suspect that it was my gender she was partly responding to. I didn't care. I could do no wrong. Though that was an irritant to my wife, her daughter, I think she realized that the alternative would have been much worse. Over the years, we started joking about it — "the son I never had" — and we had a great relationship. –*David, Spoiled SIL*

 Life Lesson from a Savvy DIL

You are a lucky guy, David. But the real winner is your wife! *–KC*

"I've always appreciated her steadiness, her perspective, and the way a wisecrack from her reverberates around the room."

–Former President Barack Obama, on his mother-in-law, Marian Robinson

Seek and ye shall find Switzerland

Once again, good food and wine to the rescue!

When we were expecting our first baby, I was in a fairly new job, and one that didn't offer any flexibility. The cost of quality care for an infant was staggering, so we decided to accept my mother-in-law's offer to come for an extended stay to help us.

She was used to home being *her* household. I was used to home being *my* household. She wanted to be useful, and that often presented as wanting to take over and do it her way. At first, we had terrible conflicts, many nights with slamming doors and stony silence. At some point I realized I needed to look at the situation from her vantage point. I asked myself, where is the advice coming from? The answer almost always was she was just trying to help.

Next, I decided to look for something that she does better than I, so she could rightfully offer me advice that I would appreciate. Cooking. She is a fabulous cook, and I am not. We started having cooking nights, where she introduced a favorite recipe and talked me through how she prepares it. We'd share a glass of wine or two. Basically, we found "Switzerland" in this activity and grew to have a wonderful, loving friendship. *–Seraina, All-in DIL*

Life Lesson from a Savvy DIL

This is a fabulous story! I love that you were able to step back and think about your MIL's true intent, which was to be helpful. It was also very astute of you to ask for your MIL's advice in an area where you truly needed it. Coming together over an activity, like cooking (with wine!), is a lovely way to build bonds. *–Shannon*

"Blood only" is as nasty as it sounds

I can nearly see the want, but object to the expression. Maybe "for old time's sake"?

My parents raised us with a "come one, come all" attitude. Sunday dinners were a revolving door of friends and family. Our 4th of July barbeques could swell to more than 50 people. When I fell in love with my future husband, he was included in our family photos, including the Christmas card the year we were engaged. So it was a complete shock to me when during his family photos, my mother-in-law did a call for "blood only." Meaning, for these photos, she wanted just her children and their children. This extended to our wedding photos too, just to be clear. In her home she has a framed photo of each child's wedding party but no "non-blood" bride or groom in sight. I asked her why, and she said it was just in case the marriage didn't work out, she'd still have a lovely photo of her and her kids all dressed up. Really?! As if she would still want framed photos of our failed marriages in the house? *–Maddi, Righteous DIL*

 **Life Lesson from a Savvy DIL**

Those are definitely two ends of the spectrum! It's hard to see things through someone else's perspective when it's so very different from your own. Your MIL is proud of the family she made, and maybe there's something going on for her under the surface that you don't know about. Practice what your loving family taught you — accept and welcome her for who she is. It's clearly not personal! Also, make time with your spouse to understand how the two of you bridge that gap. *–Karolyn*

Sometimes you just plow through and nail it

I'm so glad this story turned out like it did. "Naked in a confined space" so rarely has a good ending.

My mother-in-law is very generous, and has been from the start. I'm not into designer clothing. At all. My close friends are allowed to call me cheap. Here's how I shop: I check the price tag, I look at the dress, THEN I try it on. My mother-in-law is not like that. Before our wedding, she wanted to buy me a dress for our rehearsal dinner. My suggestion of the sun dress I wore to a family get-together the prior summer was, apparently, not quite right. She insisted. We went shopping. Into the dressing room she went with me. She asked for Spanx, "just to smooth things over." (Truth be told, that's exactly what I was thinking.) The whole thing was kind of awkward. Naked in a confined space with my fiancé's mom. She wouldn't let me look at the price tag, but I believe it was upwards of $600. And she loaned me jewelry for the occasion. This might have seemed invasive and controlling, but somehow, she made it welcoming and generous. I felt loved in those Spanx and $600 dress. *—Cady, Spanx'd DIL*

Life Lesson from a Savvy DIL

Kudos to you for allowing an uncomfortable moment to unfold, and how awesome that it did so with an amicable ending. Your MIL clearly felt this was an area where she could add value, and you (uncomfortably) let her take the reins. You did the right thing, and even better, ended up looking fabulous in the end! #winning *—Katie*

Vulnerable in the grandest sense

Imagine the enormity of Stephanie's gift to her mother-in-law.

For our first baby, it was just my mom (and my husband) in the delivery room. For the second baby, I asked my mother-in-law to be there too. She was so touched. I had a moment of regret — naked and then some, in a small room with my mother-in-law?! But I got over that immediately; it was such an emotional experience. And looking back, it was my way of returning her generosity in kind. It was also a defining moment in our relationship, giving us something shared and trusting. Vaginal tear and all. *–Stephanie, Vulnerable DIL*

 Life Lesson from a Savvy DIL

Clearly you already had a good relationship with your mother-in-law. That's awesome. Know that you are lucky. Many mothers-in-law, mine included, would have critiqued you, your womb, your contractions, and your vaginal tear. *–KC*

Vibrant and viable are worthy goals

Mel's story was so refreshing and comforting, I decided to quote her directly. Who wouldn't want to be like Mel's mother-in-law!

To all the mothers-in-law out there: Stay viable. I like being with my mother-in-law. She is interested in others and has continued to educate herself — from community college classes, to the History Channel, to the *NY Times*. When she sits down with me, or we talk on the phone, she is *present*: asking questions, actively listening and asking follow-up questions. She has remained vibrant, and I love her for that. –*Mel, Lucky DIL*

 **Life Lesson from a Savvy DIL**

This is refreshing. In every way. Lucky you! –*KC*

The best story ever

Oh, to have Danielle's wisdom to know when it's time to pause and regroup.

My mother-in-law was ready for her "granny time" alone with Penny. I had put off this moment for weeks, but Penny was now more than 3 months old. Danielle wanted to give me the gift of time to myself, in the form of a mani-pedi at my favorite shop. She was quite insistent. I absolutely, positively did not want to hand over my baby for an afternoon, but I also didn't want any confrontation. It wasn't that I didn't trust her; I just wasn't ready. My husband didn't understand and, in fact, gently insisted I give it a try. I think he was starting to worry and wonder what had happened to his previously independent wife.

So, on the big day, I took a deep breath and went into Penny's room to get the diaper bag, the formula, the blanket and the binkie. Instead of doing all of that, I plopped down on the daybed and sobbed. Danielle came in, took one look at me, sat down next to me, put her arms around me and said, "You're just not ready, are you?" And that was that. We went to the mani-pedi together, the three of us. It was such a gift she gave to me, and it made me love her all the more. – *Melissa, Gifted DIL*

Life Lesson from a Savvy DIL

Well, now I'm crying. Melissa, your MIL is pretty awesome. And, now you know you can tell her what's truly in your heart, and she will understand. She's your champion and supporter, and that's the best thing a DIL can ask for. –*Shannon*

12

Wisdom from a Mother-in-Law Virtuoso

In my years of anticipating and describing my book about being a good mother-in-law, it was virtually unheard of for someone to offer up that they had a great mother-in-law. It was the norm to hear the cautionary tales and the occasional horror story. At a team-building event at work, we were each asked to share something about our pursuits beyond the office. I said that I wanted to write a book about the dynamics of mother-in-law and daughter-in-law relationships. My co-worker Blair said, "Well, you should interview my mother-in-law. She is wonderful." So I did. Her names is Pat Christie. What a lovely woman. The first thing you notice about Pat is how much she LOVES her children, and by extension, she darn well is going to love their life-partners as well. She stresses respect and trust as necessary tools in a mother-in-law's toolkit.

Respect and trust, an unbeatable duo

Some words of wisdom from this mother of 7, grandmother to 15 and great-grandma to 1.

1. Don't sweat the small stuff. Over a lifetime, what seems so important in the moment, in almost all cases, won't matter in the long term.

2. If you have concerns, don't voice them. You raised your children, so trust them (to make good choices).

3. No matter what you think your daughter-in-law is asking you, give her your thoughts, not your judgments.

4. Life is a learning process. Remember as you move into the role of mother-in-law and grandmother, never stop learning.

5. Enjoy being a mother-in-law; it's a completely distinct job.

6. In the early years of your child's relationship, try to see that new partner through your child's eyes, not your own.

7. Wait to be asked. Give the process of becoming a daughter-in-law or son-in-law time enough.

8. Respect your children's journeys. And, for heaven's sake, hold your tongue. Judgment and unkindness today will come back to haunt you tomorrow.

CPSIA information can be obtained
at www.ICGtesting.com
Printed in the USA
FSHW011644031020
74361FS